I0460889

The Spiral's Edge

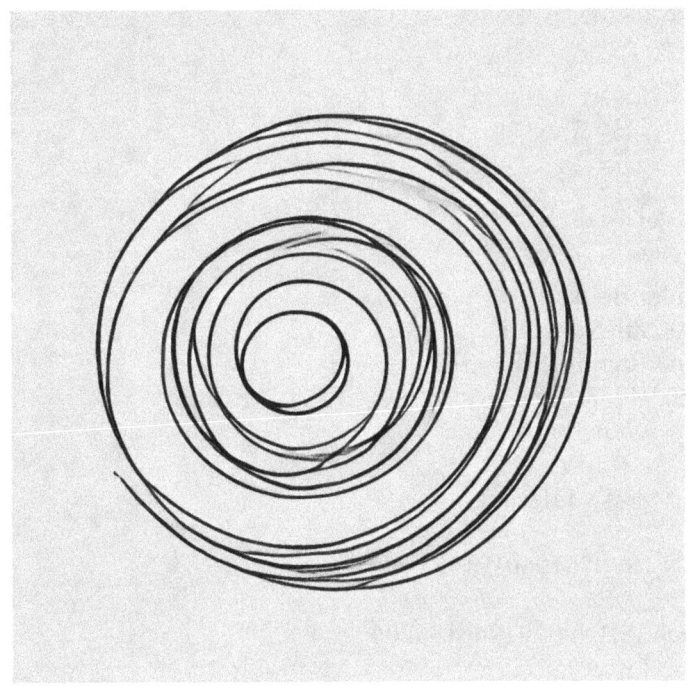

By Michael Boss

Chapbook Press

Schuler Books
2660 28th Street SE
Grand Rapids, MI 49512
(616) 942-7330
www.schulerbooks.com

The Spiral's Edge

ISBN 13: 978196619198

eBook ISBN: 9781966196204

Library of Congress Control Number: 2025903683

Copyright © 2025 Michael Boss

All rights reserved. No part of this book may be reproduced in any form except for the purpose of brief reviews or citations without the written permission of the author.

Printed in the United States by Chapbook Press.

To my Grandpa McKay, the original storyteller

Table of Contents

Ode to the Teacher

I am more than a teacher.

I listen when voices go unheard, a refuge when home is too loud,

a steadying force when tempers quake.

I bear countless names—mentor, advocate, and parent figure.

I notice what others miss: remember what time erases,

skip lunch, arrive when called. I recognize the unspoken,

the weight pressing on their shoulders, words left unsaid in the margins,

silence wrapped in defiance.

 I am more than a teacher.

I see exhaustion in slumped backs, frustration locked in clenched fists,

and hope in the slightest chin lift. I say, *Don't give up.*

Hold the line steady; teach life's hard lessons—

if you fall,

rise again.

I am more than a teacher.

I stand as a bridge, a beacon, an unwavering presence

in a world too quick to forget how deeply they crave to be understood.

I was there—

not just in passing but in the moments that mattered.

I will remember them—and they, in turn, will remember.

I am not just a teacher.

Learner's Terrain

Courage spans widening divides,

rifts of doubt and unspoken fears stretching farther apart,

Like a footbridge swaying over the fractured ground.

A terrain arises—uneven and abraded—

Steep ridges and windswept plains,

Where growth stumbles in uneven strides.

Each turn carves a new contour,

Steps reshaping the ground beneath,

as if sculpting it anew with each hesitant press,

Bearing the weight of past missteps,

Laying a path toward what remains unseen.

Through lenses honed by inquiry,

Perspective sharpens and shifts into focus.

Horizons widen, uncharted and wild,

where jagged peaks pierce a sky of shifting hues,

Where the unknown molds its traveler.

The learner rises,

grasping at light filtering through the canopy,

Footing unsteady yet firm in resolve,

Carrying forward the strength to ascend.

Uniquely One

I am a person with a name,
Cast adrift inside my brain,
A world of vision unfolds inside,
 Shapes and colors like sunlight in crystal.

I find wonders in which others see none—
Bright patterns rise in subtle shifts,
Each strand alive distinctly spun,
I am an array of senses,
 A masterpiece of strands --distinctively one.

In my concealed spaces, where awareness collides—
Too much, too fast, yet I remain.
Textures and sights, a cascade of movement,

The world outside is too loud, untamed,
An intricate whole waiting to be aligned.
Mirrored in eyes that question and seek,

It is me—a person who stands.
An existence apart, unmatched and rare--,
A baroque sequence, distinct from the known.

The River Reversed

The river bends against itself, letters tumbling like stones,

their edges too jagged to grasp. Words twist on restless water,

meanings slipping with each turn. Each page becomes a test of
will

directions smudged like chalk beneath the rain.

"Try harder," they said, but how do you grasp smoke?

"8" leans into "D,"

a shape-shifter refusing its name. And still, they equate my
silence with laziness, not survival.

The river does not flow straight. It eddies, it curls, it fights its
current.

Like my mind, it resists the easy path, forcing new routes
through the stone.

Society speaks in absolutes: illiteracy is a weakness,

a mark of failure etched into the mind. But dyslexia dances
against the grain—

a rebellion of thought, a different language of brilliance

the world refuses to learn.

Anxiety builds its dams early, brick by invisible brick.

Dropped from "average" to "lesser, "they never saw the mind

sketching blueprints in thought. Tools became my bridges:

Mind maps branching like rivers, tributaries of a single idea,

machines reading the words I could not trust,

and my voice—trained to transform ideas into motion.

Still, I move forward, a traveler along uncharted banks,

paths unmarked but no less real. For every mind
misunderstood,

every potential overlooked,

there is a story untold. And for every dam built too soon,

a river is breaking free.

I navigate each path; my steps recall the way, even rivers that
rebel

find their way to the ocean.

I will carve my maps on the current, trace constellations in the
ripples,

and call them mine.

The Spectrum Speaks

The world pulses in frequencies I cannot always decode—

a symphony of sounds cascading like water over stone.

I grasp the meaning, but it dissipates like mist, a melody
fading before it lands.

Your face is an ever-changing puzzle. Its edges are elusive,
and it comprises pieces that refuse to fit.

Your emotions drift like clouds, patterns I can't always read.

Not from indifference but because my mind constructs a
language foreign to you.

Please do not mistake my quiet for absence or my stillness for
peace.

Sometimes, the lights carve too sharp and sounds pierce the
air, pressing the atmosphere inward, tightening its hold.

My body curls into itself—a refuge against the storm.

When everything collides at once, I cling to consistency,

routes mapped through chaos, paths etched in the flood.

What you call "rigid," I call survival.

When structure falters, I retreat inward into a world I can
shape. Daydreams build my sanctuary,

where thoughts craft companions who demand nothing in
return.

I drift—not to escape, but to steady myself in the whirlwind of existence.

While you read emotions at a glance, I study the unnoticed—

the way light catches a thread, the subtle tremor of a hand. I see the world differently but no less vividly.

Yes, I carry storms, their energy spilling over.

Yes, my resting mind does not rest like yours—its fires never genuinely dim.

But even in this, there is meaning.---There is me.

Please do not teach me to think like you, move like you, or fold me into your world's shape.

What if the world bent, just a little, to hold my shape instead?

I stand unbroken; I am a variation of the infinite— a different star in the same vast sky;

my light is valid, and my orbit is actual.

The hallmark of a society is not its ability to correct but its willingness to include.

Please do not pity me.

See me.

I am here—

a spectrum alive with meaning, a song worth hearing,

a shape worth knowing.

Absorbed

Knowledge splattered—

into my eyes,

my hair,

up my nose.

It clung

where I couldn't

reach.

Unmeasured

In a room of quiet deliberation,

we trace the outlines of unseen burdens,

searching for patterns in the unrest

shapes cast by an unspoken strain.

A child lingers at the edge of reason,

their story tangled in unseen threads,

A silence too sharp,

a gaze that falters,

a world too loud to hold.

They search for meaning in a language,

not built for them---

adrift in something nameless—

no sensory flaw, no visible scar,

but a tempest without claim.

A struggle to connect,

hands too hesitant to reach,

a bridge half-built, left incomplete.

Behaviors deemed unfit,

emotions raw, unchecked—

Unexpected beneath the sky.

But in their world, the clouds don't part,

and rules bend into unrecognizable shapes.

Sadness retreats like tides,

drawing light from their form,

leaving only the weight of isolation,

the ache of the heart,

fears as immovable as stone.

And so, we ask with careful breath:

Does the storm touch their learning?

Does it extend beyond the surface?

Has it carved itself too deeply,

The team convenes,

thoughts scattered,

a chorus of voices seeking clarity,

searching for a path within the maze.

For a child, are not their broken parts,

not their worries, their wounds, their quiet,

they are a spark waiting to ignite—

a constellation of stars unseen ---brilliance waiting to shine.

Wired and Wandering

My mind flits like a hummingbird, dipping between moments,

never still long enough to hold their meaning.

Thoughts unravel like vapor, rising in shifting threads,

dissolving before they settle.

Instructions scatter like riddles, half-heard, half-lost, and vanishing in the space

between word and motion.

I try to hold them, but they slip through my grasp,

like water through parted hands.

My body vibrates in restless motion, fingers tapping, feet shifting,

energy crackling like a live wire—a wildfire contained in whispers.

"Sit still?" I attempt. But the world presses in,

too sharp,

too loud,

too much.

Words tumble before I catch them, spilling like marbles from a jar—

scattering, rolling, breaking the hush.

"My turn?"It's always now.

Waiting stretches endlessly, like a breath held beneath the tide.

And danger—what is danger?

The lure of rooftops, the sharp pull of speed.

It does not warn; it only dares.

Yet, there is wonder in this disorder— a current sparking in the dim corners.

I see the world in pulses, each moment brimming with charge.

Though my hands misplace pencils, and time drifts beyond reach, I do not lose vision.

Ideas rise like kites, twisting, diving, and always just ahead—

Always pulling me forward.

To my rhythm, my wandering blaze, my wired and wondering mind.

I am a storm.

Her World of Touch and Sound

She steps into the school day, her cane tapping rhythms against the hallway floor—a steady percussion in the symphony of morning sounds. She navigates each path, her steps recalling the way, and turns etched in her head like a practiced melody.

Mia is in my class. Her fingers dance across a special typewriter, capturing the lecture faster than I can. I watch, struggling to write half of what she absorbs with ease.

One day, the teacher asked us about our dreams. Mia spoke confidently: she wanted to be a music therapist, helping children find meaning in sound. When it was my turn, I hesitated; I said I was undecided.

I've always wondered how she navigates a world wrapped in darkness. Once, I closed my eyes and tried walking down the hall. In minutes, I lost all sense of direction, hands fumbling for walls, colliding with my shoulders. I was completely disoriented.

But Mia moves with grace, unshaken. One morning, I said hi as she passed. She turned to me instantly, smiling."How did you know it was me?" I asked, baffled. "Everyone has a distinct sound," she replied, matter-of-fact, "To me, it's like a face."

Later, I walked by the music room. The door was ajar, and there she was—singing as her hands glided over the piano keys, notes pouring out, rich and flawless. I learned she's classically trained in both voice and piano.

As the weeks passed, we talked more in class. Mia told me she was getting an "A."I never said a word about my grade. At the end of the year, she will stand before the auditorium—our valedictorian.

Before Christmas, she knitted a sweater for her helper, just one of many creations she sells on her website.

Mia doesn't just make life work for her. She redefines it. And yet, once or twice, I felt sorry for her. Or for myself.

But Mia sees—not with her eyes, but with her heart. She is a hymn, a testament to strength, to thriving in a world that never considered her.

The God of My Movement

The morning begins with stillness. My eyes trace the ceiling, a conversation waiting to bloom.

I speak with my gaze—a blink, a shift—clenching words tight, struggling to be heard.

The helpers arrive, steady but unsure. They are the gods of my movement: Lifting, turning, dressing.

Each gesture is a soft submission—control slipping like sand through hands, I can no longer command.

Beside me, the computer speaks—its voice flat, unyielding, a stranger delivering my words.

It bridges a world that would vanish without its precision.

The machine hums softly, feeding me in measured intervals.

Tubes, like veins, trace a mechanical rhythm, binding me to its cold promise of order and survival.

They forget I am listening. Their stories weave the air, laughter tangled with frustration.

They mistake my quiet for absence, but I am here, catching every word, gathering truths

they dare not say aloud.

Eyes hover above, pity carved into their gaze. They see a body still and dependent,

but not the surge beneath—the will that shapes my day beyond their touch.

From this angle, the world tilts, faces framed by slanted light.
Their care is choreography.

I did not choose but must accept.

 Still, speak in silence.

Still, my voice rises.

The day begins.

Front of the Room

I stand before them, lesson plan, on the one hand,

turmoil lodged in my heart.

Their eyes find mine—some bright, some vacant,

some yearning for acknowledgment.

They call me "teacher."It is as if the title grants wisdom and shields me

from the storms they carry.

But they don't see how exhaustion clings to me,

a secondhand jacket, frayed, ill-fitting.

I drag their stories home—hunger, lost jobs, whispered fears.

"I didn't eat last night."

"My dad can't find work."

I collect crumpled notes, hoard unspoken confessions,

mediate battles, piece together ambitions scribbled in forgotten notebooks.

They assume I control the room, but I only balance the chaos,

dodging sharp words, failed deadlines, teetering on patience's edge

as they shape themselves in uncertainty.

They call teaching noble but never mention its rawness—

care stretched thin across forty desks, a burden multiplying

until it blurs into sleepless nights.

They don't tell you that some days, you win—a spark flares in their eyes,

and they grasp the meaning and believe they are more

than the grades that define them. And some days, you lose.

Eyes surrender, shoulders drop, and a moment slips away too fast to save.

Teaching is a battlefield, but I am no soldier.

I am the medic—patching wounds with patience, mending hearts with hope.

I bleed ink and coffee, wear victories like medals,

and carry defeats like shadows.

No, I don't have all the answers. But I am here.

Every day.

At the front of the room.

Becoming the Ground

I wake to the sound of something cracking.

The ceiling watches, its edges curling inward

as if hiding a secret too vast for me to hold.

The bed vibrates beneath me,

a low, electric hum that creeps into my ribs.

The mirror offers no argument today—

it waits, indifferent. I don't trust it, anyway.

At breakfast, the spoon feels heavier,

its weight pulling time into strange loops—

forward, backward, spiraling.

Cereal swirls like a galaxy,

It spins equations I struggle to decipher.

By noon, the walls begin to breathe.

They tremble when I stare too long,

and their exhales nudge me toward the windows.

Outside, the trees lean closer, their branches clawing the glass,

waiting for me to blink. Someone is here now.

I can't see them but feel their rhythm tapping on my shoulder.

Three beats. Stop.

Three beats. Stop.

"What do you want?" I ask,

but my words scatter like marbles,

rolling under furniture where I can't reach them.

By evening, the ground begins to split.

Not physically—no one else notices—

but beneath my feet, a crack opens, endless and consuming.

I grip the couch, but even it recoils,

its fabric slick, its texture biting.

The voices arrive at dusk—not words but vibrations,

low and relentless.

They hum with meaning, I can't untangle,

threads pulling me toward answers

I don't remember asking for it.

I press my hands to my ears. It doesn't stop.

By nightfall, I become the ground.

I am the split, the tilt, the falling.

I fold inward, waiting for sleep to flatten me,

to make me solid again.

But even dreams don't know

how to hold what is fractured.

Where I belong

My world Bends,

Distorted.

Yet, within this classroom,

I am defined.

Death Mask

I crafted a death mask, though I still breathe—

a plaster shell preserving who I was for a fleeting age.

It settles across every contour, sealing fragile strokes,

As if to capture a single instant of tranquility.

Shrouded now, this cast conceals my living face,

a silent vow to hold what always slips away.

Within me, a split self stands at odds:

One side craves the permanence of clarity

to pin each nuance in unyielding relief.

The other dissolves into endless possibilities,

refusing to claim a single shape or name.

This tension calcifies within a rigid design,

Expectations bind each fragment in place.

No corners left untouched, no rebellion spared—

every feature recast by an invisible hand.

Fine threads entwine a brittle core,

Summoning unity and burying havoc below.

Still, I cradle this death mask in trembling hands,

a monument to the desperate hope of staying whole.

The plaster's calm conceals muted defiance in a world that
demands edges over essence.

For I know I cannot remain fixed

nor entirely abandon the shape I wear

Erratic Genius

Reborn from a haunted beginning,

He rose like a balloon stretched with faults—

Then burst—his pieces scattered into the void.

He knelt among torn scraps, pressing them in place,

Trying to shape a mosaic of meaning,

Each fragment bears its uneven hue.

Compelled to create, he planted a seed,

Hoping for the bloom of serene symmetry.

Instead, a wild vine clawed upward from the soil,

Its twisted leaves grasping at empty air,

Each tendril

forces itself into a form against its nature.

Driven to untangle discord,

He spoke in riddles, cryptic and raw,

Summoning a muse from unreachable depths.

But the muse, worn thin by the weight of creation,

Broke under the strain of their fraught exchange,

Both maker and made saw their purpose

Stretch and dissolve into silence.

Here, brilliance offers no solace—

An ache of unseen visions thrums beneath his skin.

Amid a color-washed emptiness,

He glows, vibrant yet untouchable,

Illuminating but alone in the brightness.

Brilliance offers no comfort,

Only the faint reverberation of vacant possibility—

A genius adrift in the space between

What might have been

And what will never fully come to be.

Absent

The mood settles slowly, a tide of ash washing over the day.

Where once petals leaned to the sun's gaze,

now they lie folded,

forgotten in the soil's embrace.

Absent from the child, Marooned beneath a weighted sky,

Lost in a lattice of heavy clouds.

Their laughter drifts, splintering into silence,

now forgotten to the heaviness of worry.

Light pools faintly at the horizon's rim,

a fleeting trace swallowed by the wind,

its warmth dissipating like a held breath.

Laughter unravels,

Strands of sound dissolve into the air.

Smiles collapse, Folded into the stillness.

The sun hides, a golden ray snuffed by the reach of distance,

its glow faint as the memory of touch.

Mind Melt

He drifts into an artificial paradise, a labyrinth of mirrored intentions.

Anchored to illusions shifting beneath him, He circles his island universe—

Expansive yet hollow. In his thoughts, distortion takes shape—Errant flashes of moments and memories,

Patterns rise only to fracture and fall. His world contracts, spiraling inward,

Fields of light fade to shadowed gray, subtle edges dissolve into sameness,

And his horizon narrows to a single, barren point. Reduced to a stripped existence,

He marvels at the terror of his abstraction, shaking with the tremor of what endures,

Waiting for a voice that will not come. his is an apocalypse of perpetual motion,

Transformed by the mirage he chased. Descending into a muted glow of fading light

until he dissolves into the quiet void of oblivion.

Unhinged

My brain is a jungle, vines mangled,

Buried in the mix of suffocating radiance,

Hollow songs reverberate in the walls

As it closes in,

Radiance and shade blur, fading into darkness.

Behind the door, I've closed on myself,

Dark-Driven ideas scatter-

Broken phrases stumbling to coherence,

a mind unraveling under its decay.

I tread a cold path, uncharted territory,

And endless route,

Its jagged edges catch my step,

The surface is impervious to touch and reason

Instinct bypasses my splintered ideas,

Bands stretched to their snapping point,

The tension builds, then breaks into silence.

And in that serenity, clarity stirs:

Fragile, dissolving,

and Fading inside the mist of abstraction and oblivion.

Anxiety Is a Room

Anxiety is a room.

No walls, no doors—just closing angles.

The air crushes your lungs.

The floor tilts impatiently

like it's running away from you.

Anxiety is a clock.

Its hands spin wild, out of sync,

Seconds drag, sinking in quicksand,

Tick, tick, tick—pounding in your chest.

The alarm blares,

a scream with no off switch.

Time slips through your fingers,

and you can't catch it.

Anxiety is a voice.

Not loud, not soft—just sharp.

It cuts into your thoughts like broken glass.

It leans in, too close,

and whispers the same question,

Over and over:

"What if? What if?"

It turns silence into a siren,

every sound an ambush.

The creak of a door,

the slam of a car,

the empty hum of nothing—

each one a promise of collapse.

Anxiety is a thief.

It storms through your daylight,

Snatches sleep from your nights,

Robs, the calm you thought was yours.

A relentless sprint seizes your heart,

while your body stands captive.

It doesn't ask.

It doesn't knock.

It barges in, scatters its wreckage,

and leaves you drowning in a mess.

Anxiety is a maze.

Each corridor mirrors the last—

wrong turns, dead ends, spin around.

At every turn, it hisses:

"This isn't the way.

Turn back.

You won't make it."

But here's the truth:

You're still moving,

Your feet press forward one step at a time.

The maze doesn't end—

but neither do you.

Anxiety is a room,

but it's not the whole house.

It's a clock,

but the hands keep turning.

It's a thief,

but it hasn't stolen everything.

And maybe—just maybe—

Anxiety is a voice.

And this time,

You're ready to answer:

"What if I keep going ?"

"What if I make it through?"

The Edge

The blade gleams in dim light, a measure of control in the disarray.

A sting, a burn, lines traced without words—

A boundary emerges where none existed before.

Skin yields, red rivers carving winding paths,

too tangled to name aloud.

Here, the ache becomes visible—counted like tally marks

etched into the mantle of despair.

In the sting, there is clarity—a moment where the world slows,

thoughts retreat, leaving only the sharpness of now.

It is not a cry for help.

It is a lullaby to numbness, a ritual of release and regret.

The scars do not scream.

They whisper.

Healed yet haunting, they carve maps of battles fought in silence,

Wars waged without victors.

Beneath the surface, a pulse persists—

faint but alive.

I trace the edges of absence, a sculpture shaped by wounds.

And in the calm, I dare to imagine—not what falls apart
but what might grow from the scars.

Transparent

It starts with a whisper,

a mirror muttering lies:

"Not enough, never enough."

She listens,

her reflection shrinking

a little more each day.

Plates emptied into porcelain mouths,

her hunger swallowed whole.

Cheeks hollow,

a faint outline fades beneath her skin,

carving away the person she once was.

She feels it first in her eyes—

the way they dim,

losing their gleam to the world.

Magazines promise salvation,

their glossy pages cutting deep,

fragmenting her self-image.

Social feeds scroll past—

flawless bodies like sandpaper,

grating her fragile frame.

Her skin thins like tracing paper,

fingers trembling as they pull

at flaws only she can see.

Her voice falters—

a whisper no one hears.

Friends glance through her

as if she's fading from view.

Bones are brittle, veins are blooming,

and a blue river is on a map

no one dares to follow.

Her reflection dims further.

First, her outline blurs.

Then, her shadow fails to show.

By the time her heart stutters,

slowing to an unfamiliar rhythm,

she is more absent than a person.

Her skin turns to glass;

her words dissolve into the air.

One day, they glance,

and she's no longer there.

Her chair sits empty.

Her space—a void,

She is gone—

not in death,

but in the fragile absence

she became.

The Endless Scene

The TV flickers to life each morning,

a movie I've seen a thousand times.

The remote is my lifeline to control,

but the scenes won't align—rewind, fix.

The curtain hangs crooked—rewind, fix.

The rug tilts away from the couch—rewind, fix.

Crumbs scatter in the frame's corners.

Rewind, fix. Rewind, fix.

"You missed a spot!"

I try to let it play—

to sit still and watch like everyone else.

But my mind grips the remote.

Rewind. Fix it. Start again.

Tension climbs my spine,

rising from my stomach,

coiling tight in my chest.

"Do something. Now!"

Rewind, fix.

"How does no one else see it wrong?"

Rewind, fix. Rewind, fix.

The voice—my director, my relentless foe—

"That scene isn't smooth enough.

That line doesn't belong.

Polish the edges until they vanish."

But the scene keeps spinning.

The world shifts and refuses to hold

the shape I demand.

I change the channel,

but the same story waits there, too—rewind, fix.

Fingers gripping the remote,

eyes locked on a screen

that never ends.

"They do it all wrong!"

By evening, I collapse,

worn thin from endless revisions,

only to hear the movie reset,

the movie spinning back to the start.

Tomorrow waits,

another endless scene.

The Seer's Divide

He covers his left eye—the world sharpens, obedient.

Light advances and time holds its breath.

People exist only once, their forms singular.

A river remains a river.

A road stays a road.

He covers his right—reality shudders.

The street ripples like heat above the asphalt.

Buildings lean toward their first blueprints,

foundations bending to origins.

A car glides past—then reverses without retreating.

Both eyes open, and the world stumbles.

His stomach reels sideways.

His hands feel too large, too slow—one grasping the past,

the other already reaching forward.

Time tugs at his muscles in opposing directions, his left leg
stepping into what is,

his right dragging through what was.

Walking turns into debate, His body divided,

his spine twisting to follow warring timelines.

Faces flicker.

He speaks to a friend, but their expressions fracture, a film reel skipping frames.

They blink three times at once—

one as a child,

one now,

one in a moment yet to arrive.

Even his reflection deceives him.

Mirrors reveal a man not yet his own—a figure with graying hair,

a boy still stretching into his limbs.

Sometimes, his face lags, catching up to the rest of him.

And God, he longs to feel whole.

To stand without wavering in time.

To touch something solid, unchanging beneath his fingers.

To know that when he laughs, it will not already be vanishing into an echo.

The doctor calls it a neurological quirk.

A brain is overworked.

He says lenses will correct it. But how do you fix a world

Does that refuse to hold its shape?

He stands still, resisting the blink.

He tries to ignore the past unraveling at the edges, the future
pressing against his back.

His left eye sees the door unopened.

His right eye sees it closing behind him.

And for just a moment, he presses both palms to his face,

shutting out everything—to see if, in the dark,

he can remain whole.

A Vanishing Note

A phrase, a word, a vibration,

brushing the edge of absence.

Too soft, too brittle—waiting to dissolve.

It floats through vacant air, a flicker slipping unseen paths. To ears that reach against the rising tide of stillness.

I reach out, my hands grasp at the air, I tilt my head,

Desperate to capture its fading form—to cradle the only sound left

before it drifts into nothing.

What does it mean to hear? And feel the loss in the same instant?

To find the world dissolving, its contours erased by quiet. The word grows louder—

or am I falling closer to it?

Its presence trembles through me, filling the emptiness where voices once lived. I cling to its fleeting tone, each syllable a fragile tether.

But it recedes, the room folding into stillness, a trace of what was

that will not return.

Hand Signs

Your hand lift,

fingers curling into a question mark,

your wrist tilting--

"Are you sure?"

I respond with a flat palm,

steady, unwavering—

"Yes, I'm sure."

You exhale without sound,

your fingers tracing spirals in the air,

rewinding moments

to a place beyond reach.

I mimic the motion,

but let my hand fall halfway,

breaking the circle—

"It doesn't matter now."

Your fingers twitch,

a fist tightening,

knuckles whitening—

anger or regret,

I can't distinguish.

Your thumb grazes your palm,

thoughts circling in hesitation,

caught between what was and what is.

I press my hand to my chest,

fingers splayed like armor—

"It's not what I wanted."

Your hand folds into mine.

The grip quivers,

neither clenching nor releasing.

Then, I let go,

our fingers unraveling

into the space between us.

I draw a line,

slow, deliberate,

across the table,

across the air—

a barrier I cannot erase.

Your hand rises again,

tracing a star in the air—

the one we once wished upon,

a memory too fragile to carry.

I lift two fingers,

a peace offering,

or perhaps surrender.

Your hand opens wide,

blocking the light for a moment

before falling, empty, to your side.

My hand hesitates in midair,

caught between the pull of your shadow

and the ache of release.

I think of the weight your hands carried—

a star once wished upon,

a line drawn and broken,

and the moments we let linger too long.

I lower my hand.

The space between us

has never stretched so far.

Blood

I bleed colors

Red for memory,

blue for the present I live.

Purple,

For the future I chase.

In the Space Between

I drift through the twilight of memory, where thoughts shift
like a vapor,

too elusive to name, too distant to grasp.

A face stirs recognition; a word lingers on my tongue, but the
bridge of certainty

dissolves into obscurity.

I cradle moments like crystal, smooth yet delicate, only to
watch them slip away,

leaving ghostly imprints of what was once whole.

Time warps here—an accordion of days, compressed into
shadows or pulled beyond reach.

I cannot always retrace the path from now to then. Choices
diverge like currents,

branching without warning.

I step forward, only to question the road—Was this the way?

Did I decide, or did time decide for me?

You remind me of stories I've told and those I've lived, yet
they hover beyond reach,

like a melody unraveling in silence.

Still, I remain aware of the ember within, attuned to the quiet
shift between who I was

and who I am becoming.

There is beauty in the in-between—a steady, flickering flame.

Though the contours of my psyche blur, I still catch the gleam
in your eyes

when you say my name. I am not a shadow. I am not fading. I
am learning to exist

within the space between clarity and change,

carrying fragments of myself into each new day. Even in this
shifting maze,

there are moments of light and love.

And I hold them close,

for as long as I can

An Educator's Lament

An intended effort—

Eyes fixed, some glazed, some watchful,

Futures tangled in uncertainty,

Armed with lesson plans that crumble

Beneath the press of the day.

Goals descend sharp and unrelenting,

I am blind to the cracks I must fill.

I pour out everything,

A well-drained dry by hours of grading,

Meetings, calls, and unspoken needs.

In the dim glow of a fading purpose,

I stand among scattered intentions.

Each student, a puzzle incomplete,

Edges rough, pieces worn thin by time.

I search for meaning in their stillness,

But the silence grows heavy, unrelenting.

The room feels vast,

The space between us widens.

The rows before me blur—

A sea of expressions I cannot decode.

My voice rises, steady but strained,

Striving to close the distance words cannot cross.

For this is my educator's lament:

To give without ceasing,

To hope without reward,

To carry the weight of the unseen,

Even as I fade into the margins.

Forgotten Words

The word slips away, unbidden—not with a scream but a
tremor,

a delicate rupture of peace, unraveling what once held shape.

Its absence hums in the pauses between breaths.

I search for them in the corridors of my intellect, in the faint
trace of a name I almost recall.

They flicker like distant stars, Familiar yet unreachable. A
sentence begins, then collapses into silence,

meaning dissolving midair—unfinished, untethered, undone.

Faces dissolve like fog, Contours blur, their edges erased.

The world unravels, thread by thread, and I am left holding
fragments of what was—

a lattice of memory slipping through my grasp.

What does it mean to lose the words that once built you?

Or find your name hidden in the mist, your memories muted,

fading like a song no longer sung?

I reach for them still through the haze that pulls at my resolve,

a tide dragging me under. The words hover—so close, so
far—their faint shimmer vanishing

into the quiet ache of an unspoken prayer.

Chronic

It burrows deep into the marrow,

staking its claim, refusing to retreat.

Each breath pulls against its weight,

routine splintering into rebellion.

Pain demands offerings: a palm of pills, the hum of an electric coil,

a whispered bargain to dull its voice.

But it falters—a fragile ceasefire before it tightens its grip.

Each step, each motion, a gamble with the body's defiance,

a cost measured in fire and loss.

Stillness tempts, its hollow promise laden with lead,

its relief fleeting, its price unspoken.

They ask, "What does it feel like?"

You pause, words brittle in your throat: Aching, stabbing, searing.

But pain is more than sensation—a shadow that consumes the day,

a toll exacted in absence—of sleep, joy, and ease.

And so, you reach again: for the cold certainty of a bottle, for rituals that press the pain's edges back.

You persist—not for relief, but because life, fractured and unyielding,

demands to be carried forward.

Concrete Spine

Pain roots itself in the night, a smolder pressing into my lower back,

hips ablaze with unrest. Rest becomes a weary negotiation, morning an intruder at the door.

The body folds forward—not in surrender but for relief.

Bent, it seeks solace, the spine locking tight,

rebellion hardened into stone.

Breath narrows, ribs caught in a grip too tight to stretch.

Each inhale shrinks, and each exhale erodes.

Hunger dissolves into absence, weight slipping through unseen cracks.

Bones ache, muscles wither—fatigue, a shadow that clings.

Blood pales my thoughts as Anemia dulls the edges of the action.

Eyes burn red, clarity wavers, skin blooms with rashes—

a map of dissent traced on its surface.

Organs murmur in disarray: a heart stammering in its rhythm,

lungs caged tight, a gut knotted in revolt.

Fever climbs, heat surging through a body hollowed by strain.

Every joint finds its voice—

shoulders, knees, heels—

a symphony of defiance, sharp and clear.

This body, reshaped by pain, adapts to its narrowing bounds,

finding strength at its edges— not in resistance but in persistence.

It refuses to yield through the tight grip of aching joints

 and the slow breath press against its cage

.

Each movement is measured, and each step is earned.

They carve space where the body denies it.

Pain may write its lines into the marrow,

but this body endures,

not unbroken, but unbowed.

The Air Between Us

What are you staring at?

You say there's no difference, but I catch how your gaze
lingers—

a fraction too long, as if unraveling the mystery of me.

I sense hesitation in your step, like the unfamiliar scorched
your skin,

like my presence shattered the mirror, but your claim remains
intact.

The air between us—dense, unrelenting—

history pressing against your throat, but you force it down,
erase it with silence.

Your hands— not smeared with blood, no, not you—

but weighted with stillness, each finger curled around a tray of
assumptions.

Muted tones, brushstrokes of distance

you never realized you painted.

I feel it—stone by stone.

A wall rises between us; each excuse another layer of
avoidance,

each refusal to acknowledge me

another unwillingness to face yourself.

What are you staring at?

Your eyes skim my surface, blind to the depths—

blind to the fire, blind to the soul burning beyond your
shadow.

The air between us thickens,

a weight you will not name.

What are you staring at?

Because I see you,

and you refuse to see yourself.

Spiral's Edge

I am rooted deep, like cracks in the stone,

stilled but restless, a mosaic of salvaged relics

Forged within an unfamiliar rhythm.

Fragments scatter, obscured by time,

Shrouded in a veil that bends but refuses to yield.

The spiral unwinds beneath my feet,

each loop an expanding cipher,

a flawed map, leading me to a trembling, untouchable core.

And then it looms—

A boundary carved in shadowed light,

Unyielding, absolute.

I pause, listening: Beyond the edge, I hear echoes—

Words of forgotten choices,

Fragments of lives still moving,

their traces slipping just beyond reach.

The spiral tightens relentlessly,

its grip suffocating with silent force.

My breath halts, caught in its chokehold,

yet still, I press forward—searching for a crack in the looming dark,

an abyss yawning beneath my steps.

I cling to the faintest hope:

That something might pierce the shadow,

breaking in to release me.

Who is this person?

Who is this person?

Spinning patience from thin air, turning disorder into calm
with a steady gaze, cutting through the storm,

Who bends like a willow in the gale?

Yet, it holds firm--an oak bracing against the tide,

clearing paths for every instinct, whether swift or deliberate,

Who moves like a compass, guiding hands and hearts?

Teaching respect by offering it first, their voice a thread of
trust woven into every child's day.

Who holds the keys to unseen doors?

Unlocking dreams with kindness and empathy, their presence
an unspoken promise:

"They protect you. They recognize you."

Who crafts lessons like mosaics, each shard shaped by hours
of care?

Who dares to sing the mundane into wonder?

Turning soap bubbles into symphonies of laughter, who listens
with the weight of mountains?

Catching every word as if they were gems to be polished and
kept

Who greets the morning with hands open?

68

Planting seeds of ambition and watering them with
unwavering care?

Who knows collaboration is the sun every garden needs?

Stretching their reach to lift both students and peers

Who looks inward, unafraid of reflection, shaping themselves?

As they shape others, believing growth is a garden that never
stops blooming.

Who is this person?

Not a magician, not a saint—just a teacher,

an ordinary human holding the extraordinary and choosing
each day,

to give it away.

Acknowledgments

To my students, past and present, whose resilience, creativity, and honesty have inspired me every day, this collection is for you.

To my educational colleagues, especially those who have shared the long hours, heavy workloads, and heartfelt conversations, thank you for walking this path with me and always striving to make a difference.

To my family and friends, whose support and encouragement have carried me through every challenge and success—your belief in me means everything.

Finally, to all those who navigate the complexities of life with disabilities or mental illnesses: your stories matter, your struggles are valid, and your strength is extraordinary. Thank you for teaching me what it truly means to persevere.

www.ingramcontent.com/pod-product-compliance
Lightning Source LLC
Chambersburg PA
CBHW061714120626
46550CB00003B/1209